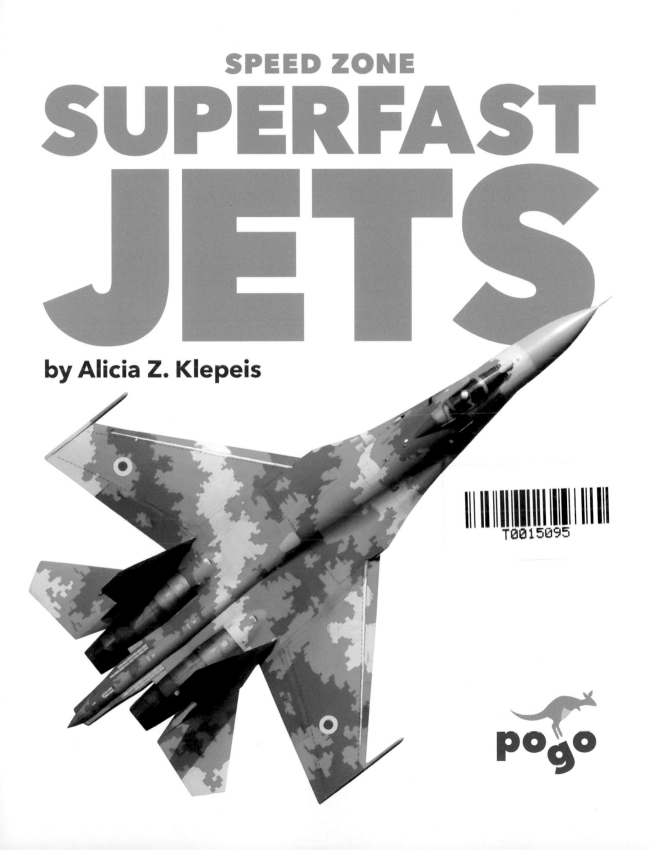

SPEED ZONE

SUPERFAST JETS

by Alicia Z. Klepeis

T0015095

pogo

Ideas for Parents and Teachers

Pogo Books let children practice reading informational text while introducing them to nonfiction features such as headings, labels, sidebars, maps, and diagrams, as well as a table of contents, glossary, and index.

Carefully leveled text with a strong photo match offers early fluent readers the support they need to succeed.

Before Reading

- "Walk" through the book and point out the various nonfiction features. Ask the student what purpose each feature serves.
- Look at the glossary together. Read and discuss the words.

Read the Book

- Have the child read the book independently.
- Invite him or her to list questions that arise from reading.

After Reading

- Discuss the child's questions. Talk about how he or she might find answers to those questions.
- Prompt the child to think more. Ask: Why can some jets fly so fast? Can you think of other superfast vehicles?

Pogo Books are published by Jump!
5357 Penn Avenue South
Minneapolis, MN 55419
www.jumplibrary.com

Library of Congress Cataloging-in-Publication Data

Names: Klepeis, Alicia, 1971- author.
Title: Superfast jets / by Alicia Z. Klepeis.
Description: Minneapolis, MN: Jump!, Inc. [2022]
Series: Speed zone
Includes index. | Audience: Ages 7-10.
Identifiers: LCCN 2020050879 (print)
LCCN 2020050880 (ebook)
ISBN 9781645279617 (hardcover)
ISBN 9781645279624 (paperback)
ISBN 9781645279631 (ebook)
Subjects: LCSH: Jet planes—Juvenile literature.
Airplanes—Jet propulsion—Juvenile literature.
Classification: LCC TL709 .K54 2022 (print)
LCC TL709 (ebook) | DDC 629.133/349—dc23
LC record available at https://lccn.loc.gov/2020050879
LC ebook record available at https://lccn.loc.gov/2020050880

Editor: Eliza Leahy
Designer: Molly Ballanger

Photo Credits: rancho_runner/iStock, cover; AMMHPhotography/Shutterstock, 1; narkorn/Shutterstock, 3; Andy A. Helbling/Shutterstock, 4; P.V.R.Murty/Shutterstock, 5; SpaceKris/Shutterstock, 6; BlueBarronPhoto/Shutterstock, 7, 17; Fasttailwind/Shutterstock, 8-9, 10-11; Newcastle/Shutterstock, 12-13; Karolis Kavolelis/Shutterstock, 14-15; SVSimagery/Shutterstock, 16; Stocktrek Images/Getty, 18-19; Alamy, 20-21; Michael Fitzsimmons/Shutterstock, 23.

Printed in the United States of America at Corporate Graphics in North Mankato, Minnesota.

TABLE OF CONTENTS

CHAPTER 1

JETTING OFF

A pilot climbs into the cockpit. He buckles in tightly. Why? This jet flies fast!

cockpit

pilot

The jet speeds down the runway. It takes off. In seconds, it is in the sky. It will fly almost three times faster than a normal passenger plane! Zoom!

runway

CHAPTER 2

BUILT TO FLY

Jets need a lot of **force** to fly fast. Force comes from a jet's **engines**. How many engines do jets have? Most have two. Others have four.

engine

Fans in the engines suck in air. The air mixes with fuel. It burns. It gets very hot. The heat pushes gases out the back. This creates **thrust**. It pushes the jet forward.

Drag works against thrust. Thrust must be greater than drag to move the jet forward.

A jet can't be too heavy. Why? **Gravity** pulls the jet toward Earth. The more a jet weighs, the harder it is to take off. **Lift** works against weight. It holds the jet in the air. To take off, a jet's lift must be greater than its weight.

DID YOU KNOW?

Once a jet is flying level, the forces work together. Lift, weight, thrust, and drag balance one another.

wing

A jet's wings create lift. They are curved on top. They are flatter on the bottom. Why? This shape creates less **air pressure** above the wings. The higher air pressure below the wings pushes them up. In turn, the jet lifts.

Superfast jets have **aerodynamic** designs. Many have pointed noses. Why? This reduces drag. It helps jets cut through the air faster.

nose

flap

Many jets have flaps. They are on the backs of the wings. Pilots control them. Flaps move downward to give the jet better lift. When they move up, it creates drag. This helps jets land.

Slats are on the front sides of the wings. When they move forward, it creates more **surface area**. This also increases lift.

CHAPTER 3

NEED FOR SPEED

sound
barrier

Supersonic jets fly between one and five times the speed of sound. Jets that fly at the speed of sound go 760 miles (1,223 kilometers) per hour. They are called **Mach** 1.0 jets.

Mach 2.0 jets travel at twice that speed. They can go one mile (1.6 km) in the time it takes you to blink. **Hypersonic** aircraft can go more than five times the speed of sound. But right now, only aircraft powered by rockets go that fast.

What are the fastest jets used for? Many are used by **militaries** around the world.

Lockheed SR-71 Blackbird ······▶

TAKE A LOOK!

How fast are some of the speediest military jets? Take a look!

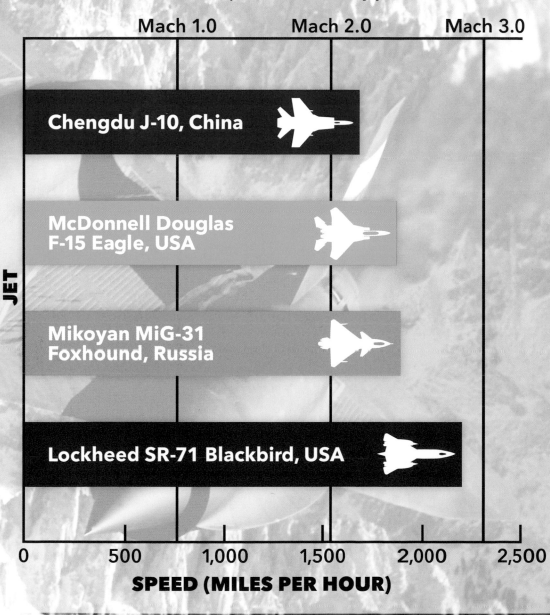

Mach 1.0   **Mach 2.0**   **Mach 3.0**

JET

Chengdu J-10, China

McDonnell Douglas
F-15 Eagle, USA

Mikoyan MiG-31
Foxhound, Russia

Lockheed SR-71 Blackbird, USA

0   500   1,000   1,500   2,000   2,500

SPEED (MILES PER HOUR)

Engineers are working on even faster jets. The Boom Overture is one. It could get passengers from California to Japan in about five hours! Today, it takes about 11.

How fast will jets go in the future? The sky is the limit!

DID YOU KNOW?

The Lockheed SR-71 Blackbird reached its top speed in 1976. It went 2,193 miles (3,529 km) per hour. No aircraft with a human crew has gone faster.

Boom Overture

ACTIVITIES & TOOLS

DESIGN YOUR OWN JETS

Create two jets and see which is speedier with this fun activity!

What You Need:
- pen or pencil
- paper
- various recycled materials (Styrofoam, bottles, cardboard, etc.)
- tape or glue
- scissors

1. **Sketch two jet designs that you think you could make and would also fly fast.**

2. **Search your home and recycling bin for materials that you could use to make your jets. Styrofoam pieces could make lightweight jet wings. A toilet paper roll or plastic bottle might work well as the jet body.**

3. **Use the materials you find to build the jets you sketched.**

4. **When both jets are done, take one in your hand. Give it a push so it flies. Repeat with the other jet. Which one goes faster? Why do you think that is? How could you make it even speedier?**

GLOSSARY

aerodynamic: Designed to move through the air easily and quickly.

air pressure: The density or weight of air.

drag: The force that slows motion, action, or advancement.

engineers: People who are specially trained to design and build machines or large structures.

engines: Machines that make things move by using gasoline, steam, or another energy source.

force: Any action that produces, stops, or changes the shape or movement of an object.

gravity: The force that pulls things toward the center of Earth and keeps them from floating away.

hypersonic: At or having to do with a speed that is greater than five times the speed of sound.

lift: The upward force that works against the pull of gravity.

Mach: A unit for measuring speed, often used for aircraft. Mach 1.0 is the speed of sound.

militaries: Armed forces of countries, such as armies or navies.

supersonic: At or having to do with a speed between one and five times the speed of sound.

surface area: The amount of space covering the outside of a 3D object.

thrust: The forward force produced by the engine of a jet or rocket.

UNITED STATES AIR FORCE

USAF

INDEX

TO LEARN MORE

Finding more information is as easy as 1, 2, 3.

1 Go to www.factsurfer.com

2 Enter "superfastjets" into the search box.

3 Choose your book to see a list of websites.

FACT SURFER